ANIMALS UNDER THREAT

ORANGUTAN

IN DANGER OF EXTINCTION!

David Orme

www.heinemann.co.uk/library
Visit our website to find out more information about **Heinemann Library** books.

To order:
☎ Phone 44 (0) 1865 888066
🖷 Send a fax to 44 (0) 1865 314091
💻 Visit the Heinemann Bookshop at www.heinemann.co.uk/library to browse our catalogue and order online.

First published in Great Britain by Heinemann Library, Halley Court, Jordan Hill, Oxford OX2 8EJ, part of Harcourt Education. Heinemann is a registered trademark of Harcourt Education Ltd.

Editorial: Patience Coster, Nicole Irving and Louise Galpine
Design: Ian Winton and Jo Hinton-Malivoire
Artwork: Stewart Lafford and Stefan Chabluk
Picture Research: Laura Durman
Production: Camilla Smith
Consultant: Michael Chinery

Originated by Dot Gradations Ltd
Printed in China by WKT Company Limited

ISBN 0 431 18907 2
09 08 07 06 05
10 9 8 7 6 5 4 3 2 1

British Library Cataloguing in Publication Data
Orme, David
Orangutan - (Animals under threat)
599.8'83
A full catalogue record for this book is available from the British Library.

The publishers would like to thank Sue Sheward of the Sepilok Orangutan Appeal UK for her help in the preparation of this book.

Acknowledgements
The Publishers would like to thank the following for permission to reproduce photographs: Bruce Coleman pp. **5** and cover (Natural Selection Inc./Bruce Coleman Collection), **17**, **18** (Christer Fredriksson/Bruce Coleman); Corbis pp. **14** (Chris Hellier), **15** (W. Perry Conway), **21** (Wayne Lawler/Ecoscene), **23** (Tony Arruza), **24** (Charles O'Rear), **27** (Corbis Sygma), **28** (W. Perry Conway), **36** (Roman Soumar), **40** (Robert Patrick/Corbis Sygma); Digital Vision p. **4**; Frank Lane Picture Agency pp. **8** (K. Wothe/ Minden Pictures), **11** (J. Oonk/Foto Natura Stock), **19** (Silvestris/FLPA), **22** (F. Lantina/Minden Pictures), **32** (Konrad Wothe/Minden Pictures), **35** (Albert Visage), **39** (John Holmes); Sharon Gekoski-Kimmel/Orangutan Foundation International pp. **30**, **41**; Greenpeace p. **42**; NASA p. **25**; NHPA pp. **7** (Martin Harvey), **29** (Daniel Heuclin), **34**, (Martin Harvey); Oxford Scientific Films pp. **9** (Daniel Cox), **33** (Stephen Kimminau), **38** (Mike Hill), **43** (Konrad Wothe); PhotoDisc p. **16**; Sepilok Orangutan Appeal UK p. **37**; Smithsonian Institution/Jessie Cohen pp. **12–13**; Still Pictures pp. **26** (Mark Edwards), **31** (Mark Edwards). Header and background image reproduced with permission of PhotoDisc.

Contents

Words printed in the text in bold, **like this**, are explained in the Glossary.

Orangutans are part of a group of mammals called primates. All primates have five **digits** on each hand or foot. Orangutans belong to a small group of primates called the great apes, to which humans are closely related. People have always found the great apes fascinating because they are so like us, in the way their bodies are designed and in their behaviour.

Recently scientists have worked out how similar to us these animals are. All the great apes, including humans, are descended from a common ancestor. Even now, their **genes** match very closely. Other members of the great apes group are gorillas, chimpanzees and bonobos (pygmy chimps).

How animals change

Over millions of years, animal species gradually alter as they adapt to a changing **environment** or move to a new one. Animals with a particular colour of fur, for example, might be more difficult for **predators** to see and hunt. This means that more animals with this type of fur will survive to breed. Gradually the whole species will **evolve** to have the same colour of fur. This process is called **natural selection**, and it is the way in which humans and the other great apes have become different types of animal over millions of years.

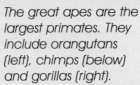

The great apes are the largest primates. They include orangutans (left), chimps (below) and gorillas (right).

People used to think that, of all the apes, only humans were able to use reason to work things out. Now we know that all apes can reason, and even communicate with each other, in quite complex ways.

The intelligent orangutan

The scientific, Latin name for the orangutan is *pongo pygmaeus*. Orangutans are orange-and-red-haired apes that live in the rainforests of Borneo and Sumatra, in the countries of Malaysia and Indonesia. Little was known about the life and behaviour of orangutans until scientists started to study them in the second half of the twentieth century. Even today, we are making new discoveries about these animals. For instance, in the last few years scientists have found that the Sumatran and Bornean orangutans are two different **species**, with different appearances and lifestyles. We have also learnt that, apart from humans, they are probably the most intelligent of all the great apes.

A female orangutan cares for her baby.

No way to treat our relatives

Orangutans are one of the world's most endangered species. Within a few years there may be none left, apart from those living in zoos and wildlife parks. The main reasons for this are loss of **habitat**, and disturbance and exploitation by people. The governments of Indonesia and Malaysia are trying hard to save these beautiful animals, but they have many other pressing problems to deal with, such as improving living conditions for growing human populations.

So do our closest animal relatives face extinction in the wild, or can orangutans – and the other great apes – live side by side with humans? This book will show that it is possible; but it will not be easy to achieve.

The decline of the orangutan

Fossil finds show that 10,000 years ago orangutans lived right across South-east Asia, as far north as southern China. Orangutans have never been common, because of the large **territory** they need. Nevertheless there were probably hundreds of thousands of them in existence.

Over the centuries the number of animals has gradually declined. In the past, this may have been caused partly by climate change, but now it is almost entirely because of the activities of people. Today orangutans are found only in the remote rainforests of Sumatra and Borneo.

Scientists estimate that the present population of orangutans is about 25,000 worldwide, with about 18,000 in Borneo and 7000 in Sumatra. Just ten years ago there were possibly twice as many. Unless there is a huge change in the way people treat the **environment**, it is estimated that the last wild orangutan will die in about 2020.

Orangutan distribution 10,000 years ago

Orangutan distribution today

0 — 1000 kilometres

PACIFIC OCEAN

BHUTAN
INDIA
BANGLADESH
CHINA
TAIWAN
MYANMAR
LAOS
Bay of Bengal
THAILAND
South China Sea
PHILIPPINES
CAMBODIA
VIETNAM
INDIAN OCEAN
BRUNEI
Celebes Sea
MALAYSIA
BORNEO
SULAWESI
INDONESIA
SUMATRA
N
AUSTRALIA

This map shows past and present population figures of orangutans in Indonesia and Malaysia.

This chart shows how fast the human population of Indonesia has grown during the twentieth century.

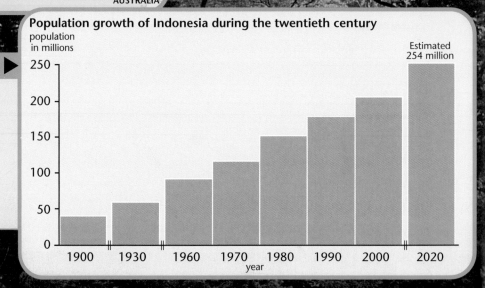

Population growth of Indonesia during the twentieth century

population in millions

Estimated 254 million

250

200

150

100

50

0

1900   1930   1960   1970   1980   1990   2000   2020

year

A worker for a logging company stands on the stump of a newly felled tree in Borneo. Cutting down the rainforest does untold damage to the world's environment.

Why has it happened?

With a mainly poor, fast-growing population, Indonesia is a **developing country**. While the orangutan population is declining, the human population is increasing at a faster and faster rate.

All these extra people need places to live and ways to earn a living. The rainforest is of no value to the people who live there unless it is put to some use. For this reason, much of the forest has been cleared so that the land can be used to grow crops. Much of what is left is being exploited for its valuable **hardwood** timber. An increasing problem is mining. As the world runs short of important minerals, such as metals, mining companies are beginning to exploit new sources in rainforest areas.

Law enforcement is another problem. Indonesia has introduced laws to protect the animals, making **poaching** and uncontrolled **logging** illegal. It cannot, however, afford to enforce these laws properly. If poor people can sell timber and animals from the rainforest to make money, then they may risk breaking the law and damaging the environment to do so. Wars in various parts of the country have made matters worse, as it has been impossible to set up proper programmes to protect the environment.

Is it hopeless?

People are beginning to realize that cutting down forests does not solve problems of poverty. Once a forest is gone, the land is often affected by **erosion** caused by heavy rainfall. Valuable forest timber takes many years to grow. People are finding ways to use the forests without seriously damaging them. But in many places it may be too late to make a difference.

Designed for the rainforest

The word orangutan means 'man of the forest' in the Malay language. This is just the right name for these animals, as they are perfectly **adapted** for forest life. Other apes, such as gorillas or chimpanzees, spend a lot of time walking 'four-legged' on the ground, using their knuckles as front feet. Orangutans rarely come down to the ground, where there might be **predators**. Only the largest males are likely to spend much time there, because they are too heavy to move safely through the trees.

Once off the ground, orangutans become remarkable acrobats. With their powerful and supple bodies, they can move confidently high up in the forest. This requires great skill. Orangutans must choose branches carefully. A broken branch could bring them crashing to the ground.

Adapted for life in the trees

An adult male orangutan can weigh up to 113 kilograms and stand up to 1.5 metres tall. He is four times stronger than a human. The tree **canopy** seems an unlikely habitat for an animal like this, as a fall would certainly mean serious injury or death.

Orangutans, however, are well adapted to life above ground. They have long arms and very flexible hip joints. Their long, narrow hands and feet are perfect for gripping as they climb vines and move through the canopy.

Orangutans drinking from a stream in Gunung Lueser National Park, Sumatra.

Why are orangutans orange?

Most animals use some kind of **camouflage** to avoid being seen. At first glance, orangutans seem to break this rule. Their orange fur would seem to make them easy to see against the dark green of the rainforest.

To understand why an orangutan's fur is the ideal camouflage colour, you need to understand how light works. When light hits an object, some of it is absorbed and some is reflected. A red object reflects only red light, so it appears red. Leaves reflect green light and absorb the rest. Deep in the forest, the trees block out direct sunlight, so most of the light is reflected from the green leaves. This means there is very little red light left to reflect off the orangutans – so they are almost impossible to see.

Moving around

Orangutans do not swing from branch to branch and jump from tree to tree like monkeys. They climb carefully through the branches and creepers, and are very skilled at judging which branches will bear their weight when they are hanging from them.

Another trick they use is tree-swaying. They move from a large tree to the top of a small, slender one, then swing back and forth until they are near enough to the next large tree they want to reach. Then they grab the branches of the new tree and hang on.

In Borneo, an orangutan uses its strong limbs to hang from vines in the rainforest.

Feeding and foraging

An orangutan expert has said that the three most important things in the life of an orangutan are food, food and food! Orangutans are powerful, active creatures and they need large quantities of high-energy food to keep them going. If you compare the life of an orangutan with that of a relatively inactive creature such as an alligator, you can understand why food is so important.

Nearly all of the orangutan's waking hours are spent finding food. The rainforest contains a wide variety of different things to eat, but finding them requires extensive knowledge, a good memory and a range of different skills.

Drinking in the air

Orangutans do not even need to come to the ground to find water. Pools of water collect high up in trees, usually where a large branch joins the trunk. These pools provide a habitat for a whole range of plants and small creatures, such as insects and frogs, as well as a drink for the **canopy** dwellers.

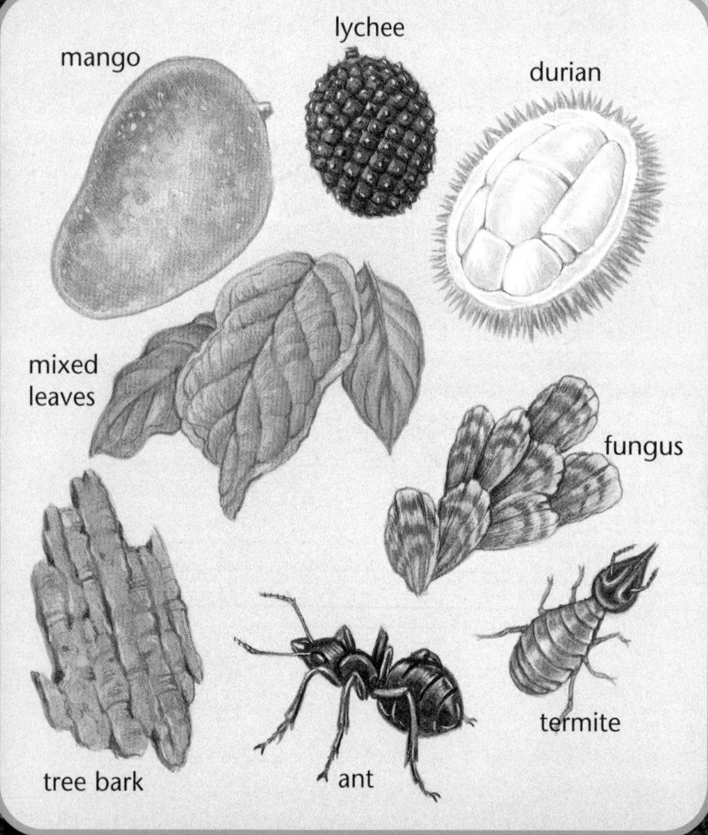

What's on the menu?

Orangutans are known to eat more than four hundred different types of food, though not all of these are available in the same area at the same time. Particular foods are found in particular **habitats**, and the animals that live there have developed their own special skills to find them.

mango

lychee

durian

mixed leaves

fungus

tree bark

ant

termite

This illustration shows the range of food orangutans eat – from fruits and leaves to bark and insects.

A young orangutan learns the secrets of feeding in the forest.

More than half the orangutan's diet is made up of fruit and seeds but it also enjoys fresh young shoots, leaves and tree bark. Orangutans love to eat termites; they break off part of a termite nest and 'drink' the termites as they pour out of it. Sometimes they eat birds' eggs and even small mammals and birds. Orangutans often eat certain kinds of soil, which may be rich in particular minerals that are essential to their diet.

Finding food

Although the rainforest is rich in plants and animals, orangutans need a large **territory** to ensure that there is enough food for them to eat. Not all food types are available all year round, and a particular tree may only fruit occasionally. Generally there are no more than three orangutans to each square kilometre of forest.

Within their territories, orangutans are **nomads**. They build sleeping nests near a good supply of food, then move on when it has all gone. During periods of drought, food may become scarce but the orangutans' varied diet provides a range of options even at these times.

For an orangutan, every day is a struggle to find enough food. If one sort of food is not available, then the orangutan must find something else. It needs to know where to look for food and how to deal with it. Some fruits and seeds are hard to open. Plants often have sharp spines to protect the tender shoots from animals that want to eat them. This constant need to search out food has affected the way in which the orangutan's brain has developed. It is one of the most intelligent of all animals, able to learn from and imitate other animals.

What and how do they learn?

There are two ways that orangutans learn: firstly by imitation, and secondly by trial and error. Orangutans are great imitators. They watch what other animals or people are doing, and then try it themselves, and keep on trying until they get it right. In this way, feeding and other skills are passed from one generation to another.

Young orangutans have an enormous amount to learn about rainforest life – the changing seasons, the fruiting patterns of trees and places where the best food is to be found. They need to have a map of their **territory** in their heads. This requires complex memory skills.

At the Think Tank at the Smithsonian National Zoological Park in the United States, orangutans learn to use a **symbol**-based language. An orangutan is shown some grapes through the glass. Can the animal remember the symbol for grapes? If it can touch the symbol on the screen, then it will get the fruit.

Success! The orangutan indicates the right symbol on the computer and gets the grapes.

Captive orangutans

It is not possible to persuade an animal in the wild to sit down and do a test, so most studies of orangutan intelligence are carried out with captive animals.

Scientists have tested how far orangutans can develop an understanding of number and **symbolic language**, and how well they can work out a series of tasks. The first experiments involved getting food out of boxes. Each box had a different way of opening. The orangutans were not fooled for long, so more difficult tests were worked out. The food was put into a locked box and the orangutans had to open another box to find the key. This took a little longer but they managed it in the end.

In another test, the orangutans were offered a choice of different quantities of grapes. By selecting the smaller quantity, they would be given more grapes; but if they picked the larger quantity, they would end up with fewer grapes. The test animals were able to reason out what was going on and soon learnt how to play the game.

Can orangutans learn a language?

Language is a way of giving a meaning to sounds and symbols. Orangutans can make various sounds and calls, each with what seems to scientists to have a simple meaning, such as a warning to other males, or a signal to attract females.

Orangutans in captivity have mastered far more than this. Although they cannot learn to speak, some of them have been taught a simple version of sign language for the deaf and can communicate using this. Others have been able to 'talk' to researchers using symbols on a computer screen. Although the results are impressive, many scientists argue that this simple understanding of symbolic language is a long way from using a language in the way that humans do.

Making and using tools

People used to think that the main difference between humans and animals was that only humans used tools. We now know that a number of animals use them. Some birds and mammals use sticks to extract food from difficult places. African vultures use rocks to smash open ostrich eggs. Green herons cast 'bait' on the surface of the water. When fish come up for the bait, the herons grab them. In captivity, a group of chimpanzees was given long poles to play with. The chimps used them to vault over a fence and escape!

Orangutans and tools

Among the great apes, chimpanzees are practised tool users, while gorillas rarely use them. For many years people thought that in the wild orangutans did not use tools either. Then in 1993 scientists observed orangutans using sticks to extract termites from their nests. They were also seen using a similar trick to get honey.

Since then, scientists have recorded other examples of tool use. Orangutans love the seeds of the neesia tree. But the fruits of this tree are covered with prickly hairs that make them difficult to handle. An orangutan will strip the bark off a stick and use it to collect the irritating hairs. It is then easy for the orangutan to peel the fruit and reach the seed.

An orangutan skilfully manipulates a stick he can use as a tool to help him feed.

Most animals simply use objects they find for tools, such as sticks or rocks. Some scientists claim that chimps and orangutans go one step further by making tools. For example, they will modify a stick to make it into a tool by stripping off the bark, or shortening it, or chewing the end to make a type of brush for collecting honey or termites.

Imitating humans

Orangutans that live with humans are extraordinarily skilful at imitating them and using their tools. Some of these activities, such as drawing with charcoal or pretending to cook using a saucepan, are just examples of play. Other activities, however, have a real purpose, such as eating using forks and spoons, drinking from cups, or putting up an umbrella to keep off the rain. It is no use trying to keep things locked up when orangutans are around. They are experts at opening doors with keys and if they can't find the key they use a tool to pick the lock!

A talent for understanding

In some forest areas, orangutans use tools; in others, they don't. Why is this? One possible reason is that tools are less important in some places than others. In one place, for example, termites might be an important part of the orangutan's diet, so a tool to extract them is essential. Another possible reason is that, like human beings, orangutans are developing. When one animal makes a discovery about how a tool can be used, other animals in that area will begin to imitate it. If orangutan communities are isolated, the knowledge will not spread to other areas.

Orangutans are now in greater contact with humans who have shown them how to use tools. Many of these 'captive' animals have been released into the wild. Therefore tool use among wild orangutans could increase much faster now than before.

By imitating humans this orangutan has learnt how to operate a pump to get water.

Male and female orangutans are very different, both in behaviour and appearance. Male orangutans are bigger, stronger animals. Mature males have large cheek pads on the sides of their faces and throat pouches under their chins. No one is sure why the males have these, though it may be to do with making their loud calls travel further. It certainly makes them look more threatening.

A mature male orangutan showing his face pads.

Why are orangutans solitary?

Other **species** of great apes are social animals, living together in groups. Orangutans have developed a solitary lifestyle because they need large territories to ensure they have enough to eat. Females live with their offspring but rarely associate with other females. Captive animals, whose food is supplied plentifully and regularly, seem perfectly capable of living together happily.

The most important difference between male and female orangutans is the way in which they live. Adult males spend their lives alone in their **territories**, only occasionally meeting up with females to mate. Protecting their territory is important and they will fight any other male who comes near. In contrast, females and young orangutans live together. **Juvenile** orangutans often develop friendships with others of the same age.

Bringing up baby

Young orangutans stay with their mothers for a long time. Adult males take no part in bringing up their young. The female orangutan is **pregnant** for nearly nine months, and her baby stays very close to her for the first year of its life. It continues to live close by until it is **weaned**, between the ages of four and six years old. Unlike many other animals, young orangutans have a great deal to learn before they can survive alone in the rainforest. In these early years they are very vulnerable, especially to poachers.

A slow breeding rate

Orangutans live for a long time. It is not uncommon for them to survive until forty or even fifty years of age in the wild. Female orangutans give birth only once in a period of eight to ten years, and only have a single baby at a time. Most females will only have two or three babies in a lifetime. Therefore the population changes very slowly.

This used to be an advantage for orangutans, as the forest can only support a limited number of animals. However, now orangutans are at a disadvantage. If their population decreases because of **poaching** or other interference, it takes many years to build back up again. Orangutan populations used to be in balance with their environment. Now the balance has been disturbed and the consequences are serious.

▶

A female orangutan with a juvenile. The males take no part in bringing up their young.

Why do orangutans need such large **territories**? Rainforests seem to be full of food suitable for orangutans but they do need a great deal of it. Most of the time there is plenty of food but because of drought and other climatic factors, conditions can change. Many trees do not produce fruit every year and orangutans may have to travel long distances to find the food they need. Orangutans need territories big enough to cope with the bad times as well as the good.

Orangutan country

Orangutans prefer lowland rainforest, near the coast. These forests are more productive than those higher up in the mountains. However, they are also the easiest for people to reach and more likely than upland forests to be cleared for cultivation or used for **logging**.

Areas affected by logging or other activities are called **degraded forest**. They cannot support as many animals as the unaffected areas. Orangutans find it difficult to adapt quickly to a new **environment**. It takes a lifetime of experience to learn how to live in a particular area of rainforest and if they are moved orangutans find it hard to thrive. This is why moving orangutans to nature reserves is not an ideal solution. Orangutans need to live in the place where they have spent their whole lives learning to survive.

The dense, wet Sumatran rainforest provides an ideal habitat for orangutans.

An orangutan asleep during the day in its nest in the forest canopy.

What would happen if orangutans disappeared?

The answer is that we don't know. But scientists are aware that every plant and animal plays its part in the total **ecology** of an area. The removal of just one **species** might have serious consequences in the long term. For example, the removal of one type of tree means that all the animals that depend on it are affected. In turn, all the animals that prey on these animals suddenly find their food disappearing. This can continue right up the **food chain**. It is like taking away the bottom tin from a huge stack of tins – if you are not careful, the whole stack will collapse.

We do know that orangutans play a part in spreading plants from one part of the forest to another when seeds become trapped in their fur, or are excreted in their droppings. However, we may not know quite how important this is until they are no longer there to do it.

Nests and numbers

Orangutans are very difficult to count. They hide in the thick **canopy** of the rainforest and are therefore almost impossible for humans to see. Despite this, scientists have come up with a good way of working out how many animals there are in a particular area of forest.

Scientists do not try to count orangutans – they count their sleeping nests. Orangutans are very active when they are awake, so they need long periods of rest during the day as well as at night. Almost every day, an adult orangutan builds a sleeping nest of leaves high up in the forest canopy. Knowing, on average, that an orangutan builds a new nest every day, scientists can work out approximately how many animals there are living in a particular area of rainforest.

Breaking up the forest

The island of Sumatra was once almost entirely covered by rainforest. The map below shows how much is left now. Most of this rainforest was lost in the last part of the twentieth century. Orangutans and other forest animals are living in smaller and smaller areas. Even though these areas are big enough to support a number of orangutans, this **fragmentation** of the forest may be a serious problem in the long term.

It is an advantage for any **species** – plant or animal – to have as wide a choice of breeding partners as possible. Although orangutans usually remain in their own area of forest, over centuries of slow migration there would have been opportunities for many more animals to meet and breed. If the forest is broken up, this migration cannot take place. Animals are vulnerable to environmental disasters in smaller areas. For example, if there were to be a fire in this fragmented forest, orangutans would not be able to move to a new area.

Do rainforests really matter?

Global warming is partly caused by cars and power stations, which pump **carbon dioxide** into the air. Rainforests soak up the carbon dioxide we produce. Without them, the world would warm up far more quickly. This could result in climatic disasters such as floods and droughts.

Rainforests contain thousands of plant species, many of which have not yet been looked at closely by scientists. A lot of our most important medicines came originally from rainforest plants. When the plants are gone, it will not be possible to make new discoveries to help cure diseases. Scientists believe that orangutans have learnt to cure some of their own health problems, such as **parasites**, by eating particular plants. Perhaps orangutans have things to teach us.

Sumatra was once almost covered in rainforest. This map shows how much has been lost during the past 50 years.

Roads and people

Roads through the rainforest might seem to be a less serious problem. After all, orangutans can easily cross them to get from one part of the forest to another. But roads are damaging because they enable people to reach the heart of the forest. Once there, people can damage the forest by **logging**, or hunting and killing animals. Many roads have been built to reach mines deep in the forest. Once there is a road, people begin to settle along it, building **shantytowns** and clearing the nearby forest to grow crops.

Some people believe that roads can affect the local **microclimate**. Forest trees absorb the heat from the sun, but a hard road surface reflects it. The rising hot air can lift the rain clouds, so the area on either side of the road begins to suffer from drought. As the forest dies back, bare ground appears, which then makes a wider 'hot' area.

The threat from logging and mining

Timber stacked at the riverside, in Borneo, waiting to be transported down river.

Logging is big business in the Indonesian rainforest. Tropical **hardwoods** such as teak, sandalwood and ebony are used for furniture-making and in building. Hardwoods are very valuable and fetch high prices in **developed countries**. There are laws to prevent timber from protected forests being sold, but it is very difficult to enforce them.

Mining can take up huge areas of forest. Apart from cutting down trees to build the mines, this industry can create serious pollution problems, especially in waterways. The waste products of mining, including poisons and chemicals, drain into rivers and streams.

The destruction of the forest

Cutting down trees to create wide access roads damages the **canopy** of the forest and allows the sun to reach the ground. This begins to dry out the forest. If the **microclimate** changes in this way, it means that the **habitat** is no longer suitable for a range of **species**. It can also increase the risk of forest fires.

The trees that are felled have sometimes taken hundreds of years to grow. When large areas are cleared for logging, the soil is no longer kept in place by the tree roots and is washed away by heavy rain. This means the forest is unable to grow back.

People working in the forest are often expected to live off it. They may kill and eat **bush meat**, which can involve killing and eating orangutans. Humans in the forest may also sometimes introduce diseases such as tuberculosis or pneumonia. Orangutans are so closely related to humans that they can catch some of our diseases.

The governments of Indonesia and Malaysia try to make the effects of logging and mining less damaging. Even carried out carefully, these industries still pose a threat to the forest, which will support fewer orangutans as a result.

Why does it happen?

It is easy to be angry with people who damage the rainforest, but most people in **developing countries** are poor. Working for an illegal logging operation and selling the valuable hardwood can bring in money for people to buy food. In rural areas of Indonesia, incomes are so low that many people cannot afford a proper diet. What would you put first – feeding your family or saving the environment?

How do you know it's legal?

All timber from **sustainable** forests is marked with a label. Look for a certificate from the Forest Stewardship Council, which was set up with the involvement of the Worldwide Fund for Nature. There are a number of different certificates around, so it is important to make sure that anything you buy is approved by a recognized and trustworthy organization.

▶

Teak being prepared as decking for a ship. Has this wood come from a legal source? Should we use tropical hardwoods at all?

The threat from agriculture

Logging does leave some forest behind, even if it is **degraded**. But forest that is cleared for agriculture loses most of the original plants and animals. One of the major reasons for clearing land in recent years has been to plant palm oil trees. Palm oil is used in many food products, soaps and cosmetics. It is a very valuable export crop for Indonesia, and provides work and an income for many people. Palm oil plantations are huge, and vast areas of rainforest are destroyed to create them.

The plantations are created by huge companies, who receive a lot of money from institutions such as the **World Bank**. Most of the plantations are in lowland areas near the sea, where transport is easier. These are exactly the areas that orangutans like best.

Environmentalists are concerned about the threat posed by this sort of agriculture. But Indonesia's growing population needs a source of income. It is easy for people in **developed countries**, who are well off, to criticize the behaviour of people in **developing countries**. The world needs to find ways of providing people with an income that do not involve destroying the forest.

Subsistence farming

Small farmers who need sufficient land to grow crops to feed their families are also involved in clearing the forest. They do it by a method called 'slash-and-burn'. This involves chopping leaves and branches and letting them dry out, then using them to start a fire to clear the whole area.

An Indonesian subsistence farmer practising 'slash-and-burn'.

The problem is that rainforest soil is not very fertile. The dead material decays quickly and only the top layer of soil is rich in nutrients. The ash from the fire helps fertilize the ground for a short while, but soon the goodness in the soil is used up, or washed away by heavy rain. It is then cheaper to cut more forest than to buy the expensive fertilizers needed to make the existing ground productive again.

Forest fire – the great haze

During 1998, huge fires broke out all over Indonesia. They were caused mainly by the uncontrolled 'slash-and-burn' methods of **subsistence farmers**. The rainforest was unusually dry at this time. This was because of a climatic effect called **El Niño**, which caused drought in many parts of the world. The fires burned out of control for weeks. In some places, coal near the surface of the ground caught fire and burned too.

Thick smoke filled the air over large parts of South-east Asia. Around 20 million people were taken ill or had to stay in their homes. The 'great haze', as it was called, could even be seen from space. It was a very serious problem, but it did make people realize just how devastating the destruction of the forest was. The uncontrolled fires were disastrous for orangutans. They are slow-moving animals and many were burnt to death. Some were rescued but a lot of those had serious burns.

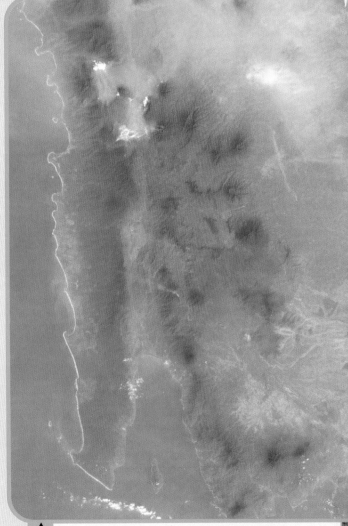

A satellite photo of the vast cloud of smoke known as the great haze. It was caused by forest fires burning out of control in Indonesia in 1998.

Orangutans are not usually aggressive animals, and they get on well with people when they live close together. Young orphaned orangutans often look upon a human as a parent, either in a zoo, in captivity, or in a rehabilitation centre. Like young children, they are good at persuading humans to give them what they want.

However, too much contact with humans is rarely a good idea. Animals that put their trust in people to this degree may lose all the skills they need to survive in the forest and can also be at risk from human disease. While animals living in zoos are generally well looked after, contact between humans and orangutans in the wild can have serious consequences.

Living too close

For humans living nearby or in the forest, orangutans are sometimes seen as a nuisance and may be killed. They occasionally damage palm oil plantations and even steal food from villages. For the orangutan, this is simply exploiting a new resource. The problem has become more severe where animals that were once kept as pets are released into the wild. Even after a long period of rehabilitation, these animals are used to associating with humans and have little fear of them.

A worker gathers the valuable crops on a palm oil plantation in Malaysia.

Orangutans – a useful resource

Traditionally, local people have seen the forest, and the animals and plants that live in it, as a free resource. They do not always like foreigners or their government telling them what they can and cannot do and often take little notice when local laws are introduced.

To some extent, orangutans have always been victims of hunters on the lookout for **bush meat** but the number killed has had little effect on the total population. However, when people from **developed countries** began to demand baby orangutans as pets, local people saw the animals as a useful source of income and began to hunt them in a more organized way.

Exploitation by developed countries

It is by no means only the local people who are a threat to orangutans. For many years, captive orangutans have been exploited in developed countries. Many captive animals are expected to perform in various ways to entertain humans. They are amusing and can behave in human-like ways, which makes them very appealing. Orangutans have become film stars and have even appeared in television commercials.

Some people argue that keeping orangutans in captivity for research is another form of exploitation. However, the scientists involved in the research say that learning about orangutans is an important part of finding the best ways to help them survive.

▲ *Many people argue that using captive animals in the entertainment industry is just another form of exploitation. Here the actor Clint Eastwood poses with his orangutan co-star in the 1978 Hollywood film* Every Which Way But Loose.

The pet trade

Baby orangutans are very appealing and at first may fit in well with human households. They are affectionate and intelligent and can learn amusing tricks. Many people think they make ideal pets, like cats and dogs. But cats and dogs have been bred for centuries to be tame whereas orangutans are wild animals.

When they grow into adults, orangutans are powerful and unpredictable. People begin to find them very difficult to control and even dangerous. Homes start to get wrecked. Suddenly, the family pet is not fun any more and their owners want to get rid of it.

A young captive orangutan with an uncertain future.

The Naughty Family

In 1986 a popular TV show in Taiwan called *The Naughty Family* starred an orangutan called Hsaio Li. This animal was shown as an ideal household pet and many viewers thought it would be a good idea to get one. A trade in illegal animals quickly started.

It is estimated that up to 2000 baby orangutans were exported to Taiwan, a process that involved killing more than 6000 mothers. An estimated 4000 babies did not survive capture and export. As orangutans have a low birthrate, this loss of wild animals was very serious. The Taiwanese families soon tired of their pets – and asked the authorities in Taiwan to take them away. But what was to be done with them?

Rehabilitation

Many people thought the answer was simple – take them back to the rainforest and return them to the wild. This was not as easy as it sounds. It is very expensive to transport animals properly and safely. People had to be paid to collect the animals, which then had to be kept safely until they could travel back to the rainforest. It was difficult for the government of Taiwan to justify paying for all this when a much cheaper solution was simply to destroy the unwanted animals.

Skull collecting

This hobby is just one more way in which orangutans have been exploited. Orangutan skulls have always fetched good prices. Sometimes they were sold by people who claimed they were the skulls of early humans. Of course, it is difficult to find skulls of dead animals in the rainforest. It is much easier to kill a live animal for its skull.

These days, people who wish to study animal skulls can easily buy perfect plastic versions of almost every type of skull. This is just one of the simple ways in which the exploitation of orangutans can be overcome.

Most serious of all, none of the orangutans had any experience of living in the wild. They had no idea of how to go about finding their own food. If they were simply put back into the forest they would not survive.

A happier scene – a captive orangutan undergoing rehabilitation to prepare it for life in the wild.

The orangutans' **habitat** is disappearing fast and many of the surviving animals are being exploited. The situation seems hopeless. Can orangutans be saved? Should they be saved? Would the money not be better spent on helping the world's poor?

The big picture

Saving orangutans is important for a number of reasons. We have seen how important it is to protect the world's climate and preserve an important resource such as the rainforest. Orangutans play an important part in the rainforest **ecology**. If orangutans survive, then the rainforest itself will have survived.

While these arguments are important, **conservationists** believe we should not save orangutans simply for our own benefit, or even for the benefit of the planet. They argue that orangutans should be saved because they are beautiful animals, one of the closest **species** to humans, and we have a duty to protect them. So how do we go about achieving this?

No-go reserves

Reserves can be set up where human access is restricted to the people who need to be there – scientists, reserve rangers and so on. The animals can live there without fear of being exploited or losing their habitat. A number of no-go reserves have been set up in Malaysia and Indonesia. In Indonesia, for example, parks and refuges make up 16 per cent of the total forest; in these areas, **logging** and tourism are forbidden. But if the reserves are going to be successful they need rangers, which are expensive to provide, as the areas are very large and remote.

A patrol boat with Environmental Protection Agency workers on board makes its way down a river in Borneo.

Conservationists map the boundaries of a wildlife reserve in an attempt to prevent illegal logging.

Local people are sometimes forced to move away from their land to make way for a reserve. These people do not always see the point of reserves, and **poaching** and illegal logging are often ongoing problems. Reserves are a solution imposed by humans in small areas, rather than one that supports the whole **environment**. There is a danger that people around the world are given the impression that the problem is solved, and so money and time are not spent on finding better solutions.

Eco-friendly coffee

Coffee is an important crop in Indonesia. Every year, thousands of kilogrammes of coffee beans are exported. Most coffee is a type called 'robusta' coffee. This is the cheapest coffee to produce, but it has to be grown in plantations where all of the native forest has been cleared.

Another type of coffee is called 'arabica' coffee. This is more difficult and expensive to grow. However, it can be grown in the shade, among other types of trees and shrubs, providing a much more varied and sustainable habitat for wildlife.

So why isn't arabica coffee grown instead of robusta coffee? The reason is that people in the **developed countries** do not want to pay high prices for arabica coffee when they can buy robusta coffee more cheaply.

In everyone's interests

Working with nature in a **sustainable** way is a better solution. This means involving local people in making a living from the forest, in a way that provides them with income without causing damage to the forest. This would show how it is in everyone's interest to maintain the forest as it is.

Rehabilitation

The object of rehabilitation is gradually to reintroduce orangutans that have been in captivity back into their natural **environment**. These may be animals that have been kept as pets or that have suffered through forest fires or loss of **habitat** and are being relocated to another area.

The first stage of rehabilitation is quarantine. The orangutans need to be kept in special cages well away from other animals in case they have diseases. This is especially important for orangutans that have been in contact with humans for a long time.

Young orangutans in a quarantine cage at a rehabilitation centre in Borneo.

The second stage is to get them used to living in the rainforest, while still providing them with food. Sometimes the orangutans are allowed to return to the rehabilitation centre itself. The problem with this is that it may be difficult to persuade them to move away again! A better plan is to set up feeding stations deep in the forest. Each day, food is brought and left. The supply of food is gradually reduced and eventually stopped altogether.

Of course, it is impossible for a human to teach an orangutan how to be an orangutan. But orangutans are quick learners and can copy one another.

Is it a good idea?

Rehabilitation gives orangutans the chance of a normal life. The alternatives are remaining captive for the rest of their lives or being humanely destroyed. Rehabilitation is not a perfect solution but it is preferable to these options. Careful rehabilitation and release can help quickly to restock areas of rainforest that have lost orangutans through **poaching**.

Rehabilitation – the problems

Orangutans raised in captivity can never fully adapt to life in the rainforest. As we have seen, it takes years for them to learn to live in the forest and many essential life skills come from watching their mothers. The survival skills that have been passed down from generation to generation can be lost. Many released orangutans manage to survive when conditions are good, but if there is a problem such as a drought life becomes very difficult for them.

Unless great care is taken, released animals can spread disease in the wild. Rehabilitation is very expensive. Rehabilitating a single orangutan can cost thousands of dollars. Many people believe that the money would be better spent on preserving the environment and preventing orangutans from being captured in the first place.

A feeding platform for released orangutans at Bohorok sanctuary in North Sumatra.

Sanctuaries and rehabilitation centres

Sanctuaries and rehabilitation centres have a number of jobs to do. Of course, the most important is to look after any animals in their care. Apart from this, they help to protect local nature reserves and carry out scientific research on orangutans and on the rainforest itself. They also help to inform and educate people on the importance of **conservation** – especially people living in the local area.

The two following examples are of rehabilitation centres that do important work in different ways.

Sepilok sanctuary

Sepilok is run by the Malaysian Wildlife Department. Orangutans arriving at Sepilok are first put in quarantine to check for disease. Young animals start off in the nursery, then are encouraged to move further and further into the local forest reserve until finally they can live independently. This can take a number of years, and reserve rangers carefully check their progress all the time.

The orangutans are not encouraged to visit the centre itself. This is seen as vital to ensure they develop as fully wild animals. Sometimes orangutans are transferred to wilder, more distant areas.

Weighing a young orangutan at Sepilok sanctuary in Malaysia.

Camp Leakey

Camp Leakey was set up in 1971 in central Borneo. It was named after
Dr Louis Leakey, (1903–72), who was probably the best known
anthropologist of the twentieth century, and is famous for his
discoveries on the early history of primates. Camp Leakey is run by the
orangutan expert, Birute Galdikas, who, with her colleagues Jane
Goodall and Dian Fossey, was inspired to set up the centre. Originally it
was heavily involved in rehabilitating orangutans and returning them
to the forest. Today it is much more involved in research.

Birute Galdikas had a different approach to the rehabilitation of
orangutans from the one used at Sepilok sanctuary. She allowed
released animals to return to the camp when they wished. As a
result, many of them have become 'bi-cultural', in other words only
semi-wild. Birute Galdikas says they have 'a passport to both worlds,
orangutan and human'.

Not everyone agrees with this approach and some scientists believe it
does more harm than good. Nevertheless there is no doubt that Birute
Galdikas is one of the greatest experts on orangutans and is well aware
that rehabilitation is not the real answer to the problems of
orangutans. 'Rehabilitation is just a Band-Aid to the habitat destruction
that is going on,' she says. 'If we don't save the **habitat**, then the
orangutan will become extinct.'

Zoos and conservation

Traditional zoos were not set up for the benefit of animals. Instead they were places where people went to be entertained. Such old-fashioned zoos are poor places for animals to live. In many cases, animals are kept in cages with concrete floors and cannot exercise properly. They often become bored and develop severe mental and emotional problems. This is particularly true of larger animals, such as wild cats and great apes. Although people can learn about animals to some extent by visiting this kind of zoo, they discover very little about how the animals live in the wild.

These days, zoos of this kind are disappearing. Although zoos still provide people with an enjoyable day out, they can do much more. Modern zoos carry out scientific research and may set up breeding programmes for endangered animals, perhaps so that animals bred in captivity can be released into the wild. They often provide information to educate visitors about **conservation**. And they may work towards establishing links with places where conservation is carried out in the wild.

Zoos now try much harder to provide a suitable **habitat** for their animals. Sometimes this makes it more difficult for visitors to see the animals, but this is a small price to pay if it means they are happier.

▲ An orangutan in a cage at Ho Chi Minh City Zoo in Vietnam.

San Diego Zoo

Modern zoos increasingly help animals in the wild by providing money and experts to help set up projects. A good example of this is the San Diego Zoo in the USA, which works with the Orangutan Foundation International in the Lamandau Reserve in Borneo. Experts from the zoo spend part of their time working in the reserve, helping to ensure that the release of captive orangutans is successful.

Noah's Ark?

Some people think that zoos are a simple answer to the problems of endangered **species**. They see the zoo as a sort of 'Noah's Ark' where animals can be preserved until the world **environment** improves – then they can be released back into the wild.

This is not really a workable idea. The small number of animals in zoos would not provide sufficient numbers to repopulate the world successfully. Most importantly, once people think there is a simple solution to a problem, they stop thinking about the problem itself. They ask: 'If animals can be preserved in zoos, what is the point in protecting the environment?' If people think like this, then the time will never come when 'Noah's Ark' can be opened and the animals released.

An orangutan's story

Tom King, a 28-year-old wild-born orangutan, was in trouble. He had taken to coming out of the forest and stealing food from a village. The locals had had enough; Tom was in danger of being shot.

Finally, the orangutan was taken to the sanctuary at Sepilok in Malaysia. But what could they do with him? Tom was big, tough, and aggressive. He didn't want to be there! He needed a large territory, well away from human beings. The large reserve at Tabin would be ideal. A helicopter was booked for the 40-minute flight.

On arrival at Tabin the release team opened the crate and stood back, expecting an angry animal to rush out. But Tom took his time. Eventually he climbed out, strolled towards the forest and climbed a tree. The team looked on anxiously, but they needn't have worried. Tom started to build a nest – it had been a long morning and he needed a rest!

▶

From his travel box, Tom takes a look at his new surroundings at Tabin reserve.

Managing tourism

In the last fifty years there has been a huge increase in tourism throughout the world. Before that, most people would travel just short distances for their holidays – only the very rich travelled abroad. Now cheap air flights mean that people can travel anywhere in the world.

This has caused great damage to the **environment**. Huge areas of coastline have been bulldozed for hotels and the sea has been polluted. Hotels use large quantities of water, a shrinking resource throughout the world, especially in the hot places where people like to go for their holidays. Airports have been built and roads have been constructed to reach them. The aircraft themselves pump pollution into the air.

A different kind of tourist

Eco-tourism tries to deal with some of these problems. It is based on the idea that if people are willing to pay to see wild, unspoilt country, such as the rainforests of Indonesia, then it must be worthwhile protecting the environment. Wildlife itself has economic value – it can help the economy of **developing countries** and create employment. Years ago, the very rich travelled to countries such as India and Africa to hunt wildlife. Today 'safari holidays' allow people to see animals close up and photograph them. If the animals were not there, no one would come.

At Bohorok sanctuary, tourists are given the chance to photograph orangutans in their natural habitat.

Tourists look at orangutans from a wooden bridge at Sepilok sanctuary.

What are the drawbacks?

Well-run eco-tourism can work effectively, and can provide useful employment for local people, but only if it is carefully managed. Tourists need to reach the wild places, which means airports and roads must be built. Visitors from **developed countries** – even eco-tourists – demand a high level of comfort. They use electricity, lots of water, and produce mounds of rubbish. If large numbers of people visit a sensitive environment, they inevitably cause some damage. Of all environments, the rainforest is probably the one most easily affected.

Eco-tourism and orangutans

On an African safari, there is a very good chance of seeing wild animals. The chance of seeing an orangutan in a rainforest in Borneo is very small. Scientists can go for weeks without seeing one at all. Orangutan eco-tourism depends on people seeing the animals that are being rehabilitated at one of the special stations mentioned earlier in this book.

Of course, the money that visitors bring can help to keep these places running. The danger is that the orangutans will get too used to having people around, especially if food is put out to bring them in so that people can take photographs. When this kind of thing happens, the rehabilitation centres just become another sort of zoo.

Internet tourism

A new idea could help to solve the problems caused by tourism. In many parts of the world special cameras linked to computers have been set up, allowing people to observe sensitive environments over the Internet. As technology improves it will be possible to visit anywhere in the world, with perfect pictures and sound, without leaving your own home!

The future for orangutans

This book has explained what the problems are for orangutans. In one word, the central problem is – people! The population of the world is increasing fast, especially in **developing countries** such as Indonesia. All these extra people need food and somewhere to live. This means that they need an income. From their point of view, the rainforest is a way to earn a living, either by exploiting the animals and plants that live there or by cutting it down to make way for crops. It is easy for people who enjoy a good standard of living in **developed countries** to criticize them for this. If they had hungry families to feed, would they behave any differently?

Orangutans have a particular problem because they require a great deal of space and prefer to live in those lowland areas that are the easiest for people to exploit. They also breed very slowly. **Poaching** animals for **bush meat** or as pets is a serious problem, but the most important one of all is loss of **habitat**.

▲ A **conservation** worker has become a substitute mother for this baby orangutan orphaned in the forest fires in Indonesia in 1998.

What is being done?

Many people are working very hard to help orangutans survive. No-go reserves are being set up and rehabilitation centres are striving to return displaced orangutans to the wild. But these are only short-term solutions that do not really tackle the big issue. Some people argue that in the long-term they make the problem worse. This is because they give people the idea that something is being done about orangutans. They also use up a lot of money. They divert money and people's attention from the main problem.

A special case

Possibly the only long-term solution to the problems facing the orangutan is that of **sustainable** development. Ways must be found to preserve the rainforest that also benefit the local people. Careful **eco-tourism** is one example of how this might be done. For orangutans to survive as wild creatures, we must find ways to look after the **environment** as a whole.

Orangutans are a special case as they are especially sensitive to disturbance. Because there are so few of them, they need extra help. That is what centres such as Sepilok can offer. They are not a perfect solution – but they are very important all the same.

Do orangutans have a future?

The bleak answer to this question is no – not unless action is taken now. People who care about the world and its animals sometimes feel helpless. What can an individual do to help save a **species** of animal, or the rainforest, or the world's environment? The answer is quite a lot. The next two pages of the book show how you can play your part in helping to preserve these beautiful and astonishing animals.

How can you help?

There are a range of everyday activities you can do to help preserve the world's rainforests and improve the **habitat** for orangutans. Persuade your family not to buy products made from tropical hardwoods such as teak and mahogany, unless they are certain that they come from **sustainable** plantations. Even then, it is better to think about alternatives. The more demand there is for tropical hardwoods, the more likely it is that illegal **logging** will occur.

Always recycle aluminium cans. If possible, avoid drinks sold in aluminium cans. Aluminium is used in increasing numbers of ways but mining is hugely destructive of rainforests. Trees are cut down to make room for the mining and large areas are flooded behind dams. These dams are used to make electricity to turn the aluminium ore into metal.

Never buy products made from the skins, fur, shell, bones or tusks of wild animals. Protect your own **environment**. Walk or go by bike instead of asking for a lift in the car; create a wildlife habitat where you live. Visit the websites detailed on page 46 to find out how.

Get active!

Join one of the national or international groups that support orangutans. There is a list of them at the end of this book. Alternatively, join an organization that is concerned about all wild animals, such as the Worldwide Fund for Nature, or one that helps to protect the environment, such as Greenpeace. Support your organization by fundraising and persuading friends and family to join.

Protestors from the environmental group Greenpeace raise banners in London, UK, to draw public attention to the dangers of logging in the rainforest.

Learn about wildlife. As you will have found out by reading this book, there are no simple answers to making a better world. Become an expert. That way, one day you may make an even greater contribution, perhaps as a volunteer or a scientist.

Adopt an orangutan

No, not in your own home! Rehabilitating orangutans is expensive. You can sponsor an orangutan through a number of organizations, but the Sepilok Orangutan Appeal lets you go one step further. You can adopt one of their young orangutans and get to know the individual because the organization provides you with the orphan's history. Every six months you are given an update on how the young orangutan is developing, complete with a recent picture.

To find out how to adopt a young orangutan visit the Sepilok Appeal website (details on the next page), or write to The Sepilok Orangutan Appeal UK, Charbury, Orestan Lane, Effingham, Surrey KT 24 5SN, United Kingdom.

Happy to be alive: an orangutan enjoying its freedom in Sumatra.

A good news story

In November 2002, reports of the discovery of a previously unknown population of orangutans started to appear on the Internet. The orangutans were found in a very remote area of Eastern Borneo. **Conservationists** estimate that between 1000 and 2500 animals live there. Organizations are already working hard to protect this area of forest to ensure the future of orangutans there.

Glossary

adapted   physically altered to be better suited to a new or changed environment

anthropologist   someone who studies humans and their origins

bush meat   meat of wild animals, usually monkeys

camouflage   way in which the colour and patterning of an animal's body make it difficult to see

canopy   the uppermost branches of trees in a rainforest

carbon dioxide   a gas produced when things decay or burn

conservation/conservationists   people concerned with saving the world's wild environment

degraded forest   forest that has lost many trees through logging

developed country   industrial country with a high standard of living

developing country   relatively poor, largely agricultural country attempting to become more advanced

digits   fingers or toes

ecology   branch of science that studies how animals and plants interact with each other and with their environment

eco-tourism   tourism for people interested in wild parts of the world

El Niño   an unusual rise in sea-surface temperatures in the areas of the Pacific Ocean near the Equator

environment   external surroundings in which a plant or animal lives

environmentalist   person concerned about the destruction of the environment and working actively to prevent it

erosion   wearing away of soil caused by flooding or wind. Erosion often starts when forests are cleared.

evolve   develop gradually

food chain   series of plants and animals, each one feeding on the next in the chain

fossil   remains, or the impression in a rock, of a plant or animal that died long ago

fragmentation   breaking up of a large forest into small, scattered areas of forest

genes   units present in plant and animal cells that give particular characteristics to each living thing

habitat   particular type of environment, for example rainforest or desert, that a plant or animal needs to support its life

hardwood   wood of trees such as teak and ebony used in furniture making (as opposed to softwood such as pine)

juvenile   young or immature

logging   work of felling, trimming and transporting timber

microclimate   climate of a very small area, which is affected by local conditions

natural selection   the process by which a living thing becomes better adapted to its environment and thus more likely to survive and produce more young

nomad   animal or person that continually finds a new place to live

parasite   living thing that lives off the body of another living thing

poaching   killing animals illegally for money or meat

predators   animals that live by killing and eating other animals

pregnant   having a growing embryo inside the body

shantytown   collection of poor houses roughly built with whatever materials are available

species   particular type of animal or plant, such as an orangutan

subsistence farming   farming to provide food just for your own family, not to produce crops for sale

sustainable   describes resources that can be replaced, or which are unlimited, such as the wind

symbol   something that represents or stands for something else

symbolic language   simple form of language in which symbols stand for objects and ideas

territory   the area a particular animal keeps for itself and will often defend against others

weaned   young animal able to take in food other than its mother's milk

World Bank   international bank that provides money for projects in developing countries

Useful contacts and further reading

Conservation groups and websites

Australia Orangutan Project
www.orangutan.org.au
Australian support group for orangutans.

Balikpapan Orangutan Survival Foundation (BOS)
www.orangutan.com (US site)
www.orangutans.com.au (Australian site)
An international organization supporting work in Indonesia and the station at Waniriset.

Orangutan Foundation International
www.orangutan.org
An organization that supports the conservation and understanding of the orangutan and its rainforest habitat while caring for ex-captive individuals as they make their way back to the forest.

Orangutan Foundation UK
www.orangutan.org.uk
British branch of the above organization.

Sepilok Orangutan Appeal UK
www.orangutan-appeal.org.uk
UK based voluntary organization fundraising for the Sepilok rehabilitation centre in Sabah, Malaysia.

Sumatran Orangutan Society
www.orangutans-sos.org
Helps protect Sumatran orangutans and supports the work of the Bohorok centre in Sumatra.

Worldwide Fund for Nature
www.wwf.org (international site)
www.wwf.org.uk (UK site)
Works to protect all wild animals throughout the world.

Useful information sites

www.pbs.org/wnet/nature/orangutans
US public broadcast service site with a special feature on orangutans.

www.orangutansonline.com
Regularly updated information on orangutans and the threats to their environment.

www.forests.org
Information on forests throughout the world.

www.4apes.com
The Ape Alliance – with information on all the great apes.

www.wspa.org.uk
The World Society for the Protection of Animals – helps to protect animals from cruelty.

Books

Among the Orangutans: The Birute Galdikas Story (The Great Naturalists), Evelyn Gallardo (Chronicle Books, 1993)
Classifying Living Things – Classifying Mammals, Andrew Solway (Heinemann Library, 2003)
Green Alert: Vanishing Forests, Lim Cheng Puay (Raintree, 2004)
Groundbreakers – Dian Fossey, Richard and Sarah Wood (Heinemann Library, 2001)
Living Things – Survival and Change, Steve Parker (Heinemann Library, 2000)
Nature Files – Animal Families, Anita Ganeri (Heinemann Library, 2003)
Orangutans, Wizards of the Rain Forest, Anne E. Russon (Robert Hale, 2000)
Orangutan Odyssey, Birute Galdikas, Nancy Briggs and Jane Goodall (Harry N. Abrams Inc., 1999)

Videos

In the Wild: Orangutans with Julia Roberts (PBS Home Video, USA, 2002)
Orangutans: The High Society (Discovery Channel, USA, 1998)
David Attenborough's World of Wildlife 2 – Great Apes (BBC Worldwide, UK, 1995)

Index

Titles in the *Animals under Threat* series include:

Hardback   0 431 18902 1

Hardback   0 431 18903 X

Hardback   0 431 18904 8

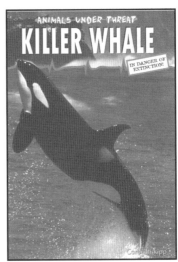

Hardback   0 431 18905 6

Hardback   0 431 18906 4

Hardback   0 431 18907 2

Find out about the other titles in this series on our website www.heinemann.co.uk/library